Moments of Reflection

Heidemarie Wawrzyn

Moments of Reflection

Bibliografische Information der Deutschen Nationalbibliothek:
Die Deutsche Nationalbibliothek verzeichnet diese Publikation in der
Deutschen Nationalbibliografie; detaillierte bibliografische Daten
sind im Internet über http://dnb.dnb.de abrufbar.

Herstellung und Verlag:
BoD - Books on Demand, Norderstedt, Germany

ISBN: 9783749464838

Preface: About the Author

Heidemarie Wawrzyn grew up in Berlin, Germany and studied History of Religions at the University of Bremen. In 1998, she received a doctorate degree for her research on antisemitism in the early German women's movement.

A few months later, in 1999, she moved to Jerusalem where she worked at different German and Jewish institutes. She became a postdoctoral researcher at the Hebrew University of Jerusalem in 2001 and a freelance transcriber of old German handwritten documents. Until her retirement in 2016, she was employed by the L. A. Mayer Museum for Islamic Art in West Jerusalem.

The present book, *Moments of Reflection,* mirrors the author's thoughts and feelings about Israel and Germany as well as her new ideas, hopes and views on nature, life and the universe.

Storyland

I have no motherland.

I have no fatherland.

Instead I got a holy land

And within, my own private storyland.

(Inspired by Elif Shafak, author of *Three Daughters of Eve,* Penguin Books, 2016, p. 367.)

Morning in Jerusalem, flock of sheep

Every Morning, a Day of Creation

Every morning is like a day of creation.

The wet, gray sky turns bright and light.

The rising sun wakes up Mother Earth.

Flowers welcome the first rays of the dawn.

Buds open up to the new warm sunlight.

Leaves dance to the tune of the morning breeze.

The quiet of the night turns into music.

The song of the birds rises to heaven,

And hopeful hearts praise the newly created day.

The Great Silence

Silence dwells inside me

Like a good companion, like a close friend.

It guides me through my day and life

And comforts me in troubled times.

Silence dwells inside me

Like a flower which wants to grow.

When it meets more stillness around,

It starts joyfully vibrating and singing.

Silence dwells inside me

Like a breathing part of something whole.

When it tastes the quiet of the desert,

It feels like walking home into the Great Silence.

(Trip to the Dead Sea, 2014).

Dead Sea, Ein Bokek

Jerusalem, March 2018

The Power of Life

Little red flowers in the desert.

Green leaves of grass on an asphalt street.

A purple flower bud in a crack of a wall.

This is the power of life.

The power of life survives against all odds.

It never ends; it is like a circle – timeless, endless.

The dots are changing but the circle remains.

Open your heart to the power of life.

Life is Life

Life is life.
It has its own speed and time,
Its rhythmic ups and downs.

Surrender to the stream of life,
Dance with its waves up and down,
And trust its wings to carry you home.

Ein Gedi, Kibbutz Hotel

Early morning in Jerusalem

While the sky is still gray and the night says
      goodbye to the universe,
The first rays of sunlight open up the dawn
      like a beautiful stage play:

Birds welcome the new day,
      filling the air with their sweet melodies.
Cats quietly stroll home, highlighting
      the peacefulness of this moment.
Pigeons gracefully walk along the empty street,
      looking for grain and seeds.

While the sky is still gray and the night says
        goodbye to the universe,
My neighbors are still asleep; no cars pass by,
        no pedestrians, no kids playing.
Only here and there, a religious man makes his
        way to the Morning Prayer.

My soul inhales the pure clearness
        and the refreshing quiet of the moment.
I ask the Holy Harmony to stay with me
        and accompany me through the day.

Mountains, Judean Desert

When I saw you for the first time,
I found you very ugly and boring.
You and your siblings all looked the same to me.

When I visited you more often
At different seasons, days and hours,
I saw you change your face like a colored veil.

When I visited you more often,
I began to pay attention to your fine features.
I noticed your different shapes and was amazed.

Mountains, Judean Desert

When I visited you more often,
I started wondering about your beginnings,
About your ancient story and endless changes.

How many centuries of history have you seen?
How many stormy times have you survived?
You are still here, filled with strength and energy.

In the Desert

At a special place on earth,
Moses and Brother Aaron received their mission.
The People of Israel found their way to freedom.
St. John helped men to rethink their way of life,
Rabbi Jesus resisted the inner and outer demons.

At the special place on earth,
We can encounter peaceful silence and freedom,
We can open up for a new beginning,
We can reach our inner place of creativity,
We even might see how heaven touches earth.

View from the Fortress Masada

Mediterranean Sea, Jaffa
(Courtesy of Donna Schatz)

Thoughts at the Seaside

Galei Yam, Galei Yam,*
Where are you coming from? Where are you going to?
What keeps you moving and changing day-in, day-out?

Galei Yam, Galei Yam,
You seem to be endless, without borders and limits.
You seem to move from horizon and to horizon.

Galei Yam, Galei Yam,
Sometimes you are peaceful and calm.
Sometimes you are roaring and sweeping.

Galei Yam, Galei Yam,
A symbol of life, freedom and death,
One day I will be part of you, enjoying your infinity.

* Galei Yam = sea waves

Die before You Die

I watched Mother Nature
And observed her circle of life:
I enjoy the return of each season.
I celebrate the beginning of every new year.

I witnessed the birth of newborn babies.
I went to the funeral of my parents.
Life seems to come and go and never end.
I am part of the eternal energy of life.

My body will rot, my brain dissolve.
But the sparkle of energy will go on and on
To keep life alive forever and ever.
Die before you die, accept the great circle of life.

A Special Friend

One day you appeared at my door.
You did not speak my language
But your eyes talked to me.
You touched my soul and I let you in –
Into my home, into my life.

We learned to understand each other,
Not by language, but by looks and gestures.
You did not ask for much.
I provided you with food and attention
And you rewarded me with tender purring.

But now the time has come to say goodbye.
I watch you getting weaker and weaker.
You are already on your way into another world.
Like a hero, you are taking it without any fear.
See you soon, my special Friend.

(In memory of my cat, 2015)

My beloved cat

End the War!

The entire world calls,
"End the war, end the war!
No more pictures of dead children!
No more images of suffering women!
No more footage of bombs and missiles!"

"End the war, end the war!"
But how and when and what comes next?
Reports on playing children in Gaza and Ashdod?
Blooming landscapes at both ends of the tunnels?
Growing seeds of tolerance and trust?

Sorry, World.
I am afraid and scared we have a long way to go.
I shed my tears.

Peace from Below

Peace from above does not work
Because peace is like a plant;
It can only grow from below.
It needs to be nurtured with soil, light, and water.

Peace grows from below
If you water it with a daily portion of hope,
If you provide a quiet, friendly environment
Far away from noisy media and ruthless leaders.

Peace begins at the pulse of daily life
Among people like you and me.

The Reed Flute

Have you ever listened to the sound of a nay?
A reed flute beautifully played by a musician?
It sounds like a soft voice coming from far away,
Bringing the sound of the desert into our world,
Making us hear the wind that touches the sand.

Have you ever listened to the sound of a nay?
A woodwind instrument, performed by a flautist?
It makes our soul travel from reality to fantasy,
Guiding us to an imaginary place of freedom,
Making us inhale the wind that touches the desert.

Have you ever listened to the sound of a nay?
The sacred musical instrument of the dervish?
It arouses our attention, makes us forget our fears,
Drawing us into the center of meditation,
Making us feel the wind that touches our Self.

Inspired by a musical event at the L. A. Mayer Museum
for Islamic Art in Jerusalem in 2014 and by Rumi's poem
The Song of the Reed (Mathnawi I, 1-35).

Chamsin

Chamsin, I love when you visit us.

While the breeze of spring makes me feel chilly,

You make me feel like wrapped in a soft shawl.

Your breeze touches my face, hands and arms.

Your warm air dances around my legs and feet.

Chamsin, I love when you visit us.

You make me feel like a little baby in a bathtub.

You keep me warm from dawn to the last sunray.

At the end of the day, I would like to say goodbye

But you always disappear as fast as you arrived.

The Buddhist

Out of the blue,
In the early hours of a new day,
A young woman appears in front of my garden,
Dressed in Buddhist clothes,
Calm and peace all around her.

Out of the blue,
In the early hours of Jerusalem,
I feel touched by lightness and joy.
Greeting the unexpected visitor,
I receive a beautiful smile in response.

Out of the blue,
In the early hours of quiet and empty streets,
The unknown Buddhist continues her way,
Leaving me behind with wonder:
Has an angel passed my home?

(Dead Sea)

Germany!

Why do I not want to visit you?
Why do I fear to enter your territory?

Returning to you is
Like submerging myself into a bad atmosphere,
Like inhaling some poisoned air,
Like walking under a constantly gray cloud.

Coming back to you is
Like encountering invisible monsters:
The past, the bad consciousness of the people,
The question how all this could happen.

At the airport, an official checks my passport,
No friendly word, no smile.
The subway trains are always on time.
The loudspeakers shout "Zurückbleiben!"
And everybody follows the instruction.

Good friends, polite people, a few sunny days,
Cultural treasures and educational institutes
Are not enough to forget your past and ghosts.

Thoughts at a Jewish Cemetery

in Berlin

Germany,
What did you do to yourself
When you slaughtered millions of your people?

You cut yourself off from sophisticated men.
You reduced your society to uniformity.
You preferred order and homogeneity.

Germany,
You scare me.

(Trip to Berlin in 2014)

Gray Clouds

Gray clouds approach my mind
When I think of Germany.
Gray clouds filled with her past and memories,
Gray clouds packed with sadness and heaviness.

Gray clouds approach my mind
When I picture her order and inflexibility,
When I remember her people's mentality
Focusing on safety, pension, and politeness.

Gray clouds approach my mind
When I feel how she contradicts my idea of life,
A labyrinth of rules, a spider's web of angst,
And always the goal of life in mind – retirement.

I do not want these clouds anymore.
I prefer vivid life, full of change and innovation,
Life with new beginnings and endings,
Life that is alive - with freedom, hope and dreams.

Flowers in Jerusalem-Baka

Going on a Trip

Going on a trip
Is like stepping out of a box.
It makes you leave the pattern of your daily life,
It helps you stretch your heart to new horizons.

Going on a trip
Is like entering an unknown area.
It refreshes your mind with new ideas and insights.
It inspires your heart with new friends and songs.

Going on a trip
Is like the beginning of a re-evaluation.
It makes you see your life in a different light.
You depart to arrive at the essence of life.

(Inspired by Maryam Mafi, author of *A little Book of Mystical Secrets*, Hampton Roads Publ., 2017, pp. 13-16).

Touched by Eternity

Eternity touches us,

When a baby is born,

When a man passes away.

Eternity touches us,

When we listen to the silence of the desert,

When the first sunray meets our face.

Eternity touches us,

When our song rises to the top of the synagogue

When the quiet of Shabbat enters our heart.

The Universe is my Home

The universe is my home,

My starting point and destination.

Mother Nature is my family:

Clouds and birds, flowers and trees.

Touched by mysterious energies,

We will travel forever together

In circles and spirals, in darkness and light

As passengers of Nature, as travelers of Life.

Pictures:

Page 22:   Photograph "Mediterranean Sea, Jaffa, 2018"

Courtesy of Donna Schatz, photographer and filmmaker, Richmond, Virginia, USA.

All other images were taken from the author's private photo collection.